English edition first published 2019 by order of the Tate Trustees
by Tate Publishing, a division of Tate Enterprises Ltd,
Millbank, London SW1P 4RG
www.tate.org.uk/publishing

First published in French as *L'atelier Papier* © Mango jeunesse, Paris, 2018
This English edition © Tate 2019

A catalogue record for this book is available from the British Library

ISBN 978 1 84976 651 7

Distributed in the United States and Canada by ABRAMS, New York
Library of Congress Control Number applied for

Printed and bound in Latvia by Jelgavas

MY DIY AFTERNOON

PAPER

l'atelier Terrains Vagues

All three of us live in Strasbourg and work together in our brilliant workshop.

Our job is to create posters and books! We also love to invent smart games for kids and fun, easy-to-follow crafts with paper, recycled materials and nature.

Our creations are colourful and geometric – it's our trademark design!

We love to work with children because we love their imaginations and their way of seeing the world.

Ambre, Marisol et Elsa
l'atelier Terrains Vagues

CONTENTS

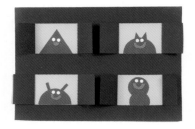

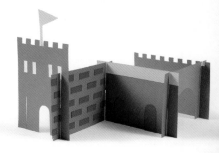

INTRODUCTION

In this book, there are eight activities
that can be made with paper.

We will show you how to make amazing creations out of paper: pop-up cards, games, castles and more – all easy to make in just a few steps! However, do not hesitate to ask for help from an adult with anything that seems a little too complicated, and always be sure to ask an adult for help when you need to use scissors or a craft knife. All of these projects can be made with tools that you can find in your school supplies, or that can be bought in a hobby or stationery store. You should feel free to improvise, and think of new ways to use the skills you'll learn in these projects.

Some tips before you start :

• For each of these crafts we use white or coloured paper, A4 size (type Canson 160 g). We advise you to use only five different paper colours to make all creations: red, dark blue, light blue, yellow and white.

• For some crafts, we will tell you to use thicker paper (type Canson 240 g). If you don't have any, you can also stick two sheets regular together to make them stiffer.

• Throughout this book, you will see that we mainly use geometric shapes to make and decorate the paper objects. You can also draw shapes by tracing around an object like a bowl, a box or a roll of tape.

• Be careful not to use too much glue, or it may overflow and make a mess of your creation!

• Always ask an adult for help when using scissors, glue or a craft knife.

There are so many different shapes and crafts that you can make with paper. Use your imagination and try out different things on your own model. If you are not satisfied with the final result, that's no problem – just take a new sheet of paper and start again!

To your papers! Ready, set . . . let's start the workshops!

HARDWARE and TOOLS

MY ANIMATED FACE

MY ANIMATED FACE

Make a paper face! Happy, shy, surprised, angry – change their expression to whatever you like!

YOU WILL NEED

- thick paper in different colours
- white paper
- a pair of scissors
- an eraser
- a pencil
- glue
- a compass
- paper fasteners

1

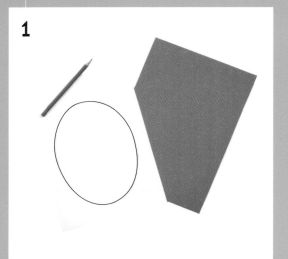

1. Draw the shape of a face on a sheet of white paper and cut it out, then stick it on to a sheet of coloured paper.
2. Draw eyes, a mouth, a nose and eyebrows on some different coloured paper then cut them out, and place them where you want them on the face.
3. Using the compass, carefully make a hole in the paper elements that you want to animate and then fix them together with paper fasteners. Fix the other elements to the face with glue.

2

3

And now you can play with your character by changing their expression!

LANDSCAPE SCENERY

LANDSCAPE SCENERY

Imagine and create a beautiful landscape that stands up by itself – just using paper!

YOU WILL NEED
- coloured paper
- a large sheet of thick coloured paper (A3)
- a pair of scissors
- an eraser
- glue
- a ruler

1

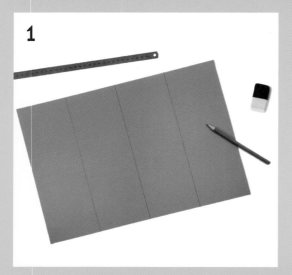

2

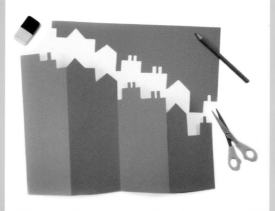

3

1. Measure out four equal bands on the A3 sized paper and then fold the paper accordion-style.
2. Draw the silhouette of a city across the page, then cut it out following the lines you have drawn.
3. Draw the different elements of the landscape onto the different coloured sheets of paper, then cut them out and glue them on the sheet to create your landscape scene.

That's it, you made a landscape!
Now you can use it as a backdrop for games.

a little tip
You can decorate both sides of the paper to create an even bigger world!

MIX-AND-MATCH MONSTERS

Make a couple of sets of these paper cards and mix them up. You can create so many different characters! Be sure to ask an adult for help with this activity.

YOU WILL NEED

- thick paper in different colours
- a pair of scissors
- a craft knife
- an eraser
- a pencil
- glue
- a ruler

1

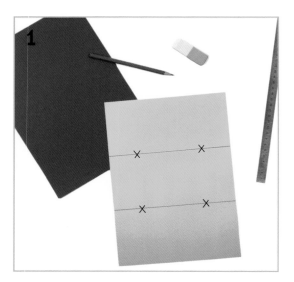

2

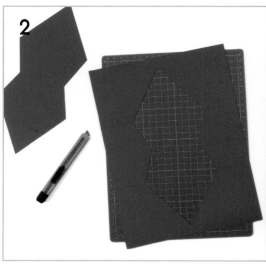

3

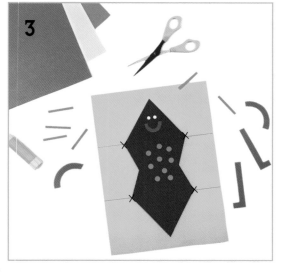

4

1. With the ruler and pencil, draw two lines to separate the paper into three equal strips, then draw four symmetrical marks on the two lines. These will be your guide marks.
2. Draw a monster's body following the guide marks, then ask an adult to cut it out with the craft knife.
3. Glue the shape on top of the marks. Draw and cut the arms, legs and faces out of coloured paper to create your character. Make sure they don't go over the lines!
4. Cut your card into three parts by following the lines you have drawn. Now you can mix them up!

a little tip
You can also make a character with more than three pieces!

Have fun creating other cards from different shapes. You can mix them up to make lots of fun characters!

POP-UP HOUSE

POP-UP HOUSE

Make yourself an easy pop-up in house in three steps!

YOU WILL NEED
- a sheet of thick coloured paper
- different coloured paper
- a pair of scissors
- an eraser
- a pencil
- glue

1. Fold the thick coloured paper sheet in half, then use a ruler to cut two parallel slits of the same length.
2. Unfold the sheet and pull the cut part inward, then push up the (dotted) folds to form a pop-up.
3. Decorate the front of your house by cutting out a door, windows, a roof and anythig else you can think of of in coloured paper, then glue them on.

Build lots of different types of houses to create a village!

a little tip
You can cut a real door in the wall
of your house!

29

CHANGING FACES

Make a paper character to express your every emotion! Be sure to ask an adult for help with this activity.

YOU WILL NEED

- thick coloured paper
- a pair of scissors
- a pencil and an eraser
- paper fasteners
- glue
- a craft knife
- a compass

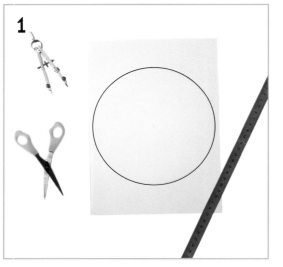

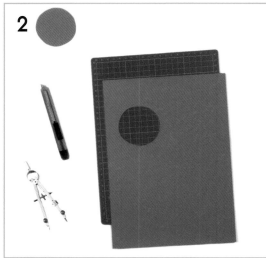

1. Using a compass, draw a 20 cm diameter circle on a sheet of paper and cut it out.
2. Draw a smaller circle on a red sheet (about 7 cm in diameter), and cut it out leaving the surrounding sheet intact.
3. Place the white circle under the red paper (making sure it pokes out from behind the red so that you can turn it) and secure the set with a paper fastener.
4. Cut out four faces from paper, each with a different expression, rotating the wheel a 1/4 turn between each face. Complete the body of your character with elements cut from coloured paper.

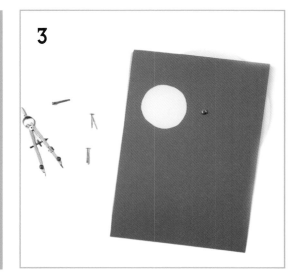

Turn the wheel to change your character's expression!

4

a little tip

You can also draw on the faces of your character with coloured markers!

LANDSCAPE IN 3D

LANDSCAPE IN 3D

Cut some simple shapes from a sheet of paper and create a landscape that comes alive! Be sure to ask an adult for help with this activity.

YOU WILL NEED

- thick coloured paper
- a pair of scissors
- an eraser
- a pencil
- glue
- a craft knife
- a compass

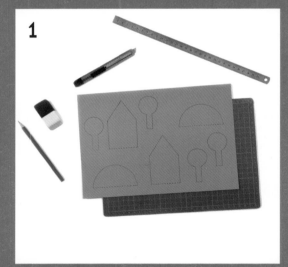

1. Take a piece of paper, and draw the outlines of your houses, trees and bushes, spaced out to fill the paper. Make sure each one has a straight base line at the bottom. With the help of an adult, use a craft knife to cut around all sides of the shapes except for the base line.

2. Fold-up each shape, so it stands up from the piece of paper, then decorate with different coloured windows, doors and other details, cut from the other sheets of paper.

3. Glue your 3D landscape onto another sheet of paper in a different colour.

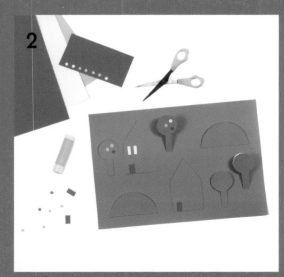

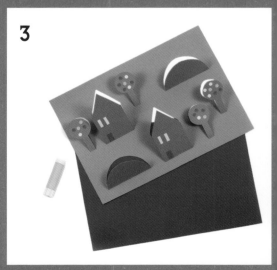

You can put different landscapes side by side
and create a real playground for your toys!

a little tip

You can use different shaped hole
punches to cut out the details.

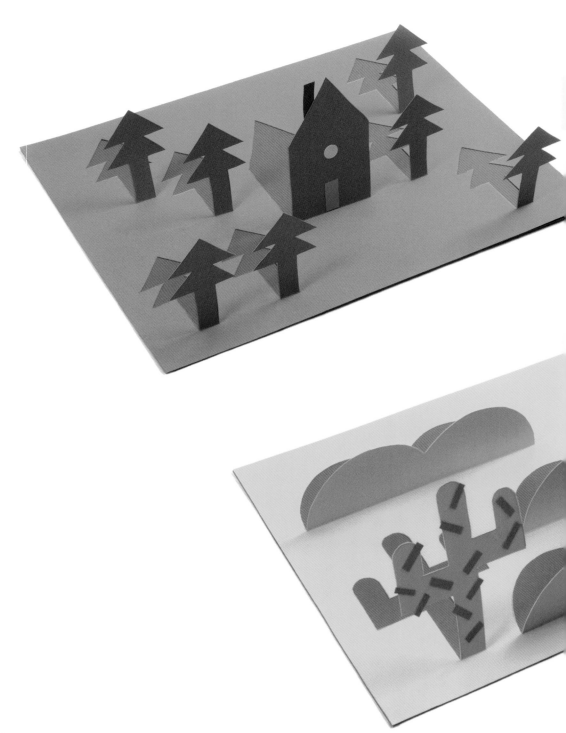

SHUTTER SURPRISE

SHUTTER SURPRISE

Make a card with shutters that hide lots of surprises!

YOU WILL NEED

- thick and normal coloured paper
- a pair of scissors
- an eraser
- a pencil
- glue
- a ruler

1

2

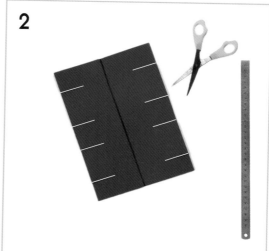

3

4

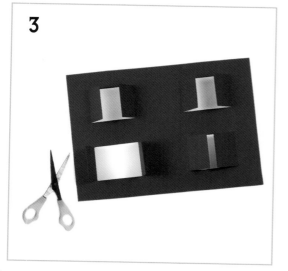

What will you find behind the shutters? It's up to you!

1. Fold a sheet of dark, heavy paper by folding both sides into the center.
2. Mark out, then cut four symetrical slits on each side.
3. Unfold the sides and cut down the center of the flaps, then fold them back to form the shutters.
4. Place the cut sheet on a sheet of light coloured paper and trace the outline of the windows in pencil. Decorate and animate each window with elements cut out of coloured paper, then glue the sheet with the shutters on top.

a little tip

You can make as many windows and doors as you like, depending on how many cuts you make. You can also hide a surprise message behind the shutters, to send to your friends!

49

BUILD-YOUR-OWN CASTLE

BUILD-YOUR-OWN CASTLE

Design your own building game! Make lots of different types of walls and you can create your own fortress.

YOU WILL NEED

- a thick sheet of paper
- coloured paper
- a pair of scissors
- an eraser
- a pencil
- glue
- a ruler

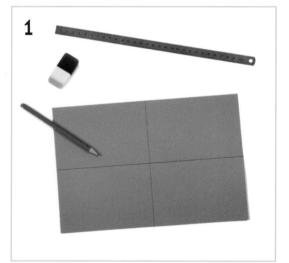

1

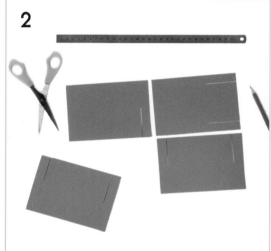

2

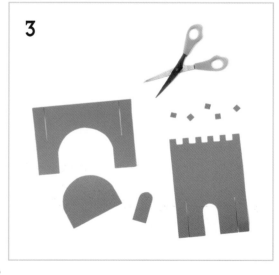

3

4

Have fun assembling the walls in different ways to create a new castle and invent a new story!

a little tip

The more walls you build,
the more your castle will grow!

1. Separate the sheet of thick paper in four equal parts and cut them out.

2. Trace and cut two slots of 6 cm length on each part, about 1 cm in from each end.

3. Draw and cut the silhouettes of the buildings and walls of your castle.

3. Cut out windows, doors and patterns out of paper and then glue the decorative elements on the walls of your castle. Now you can start to slot them together and start building!

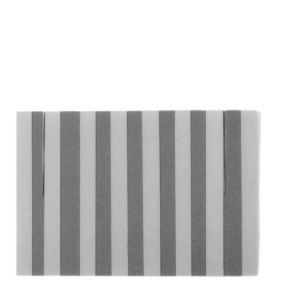

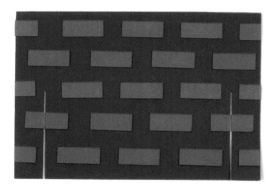

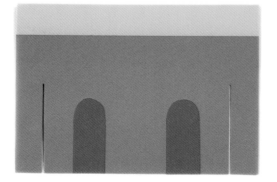

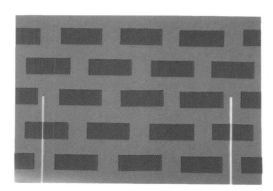

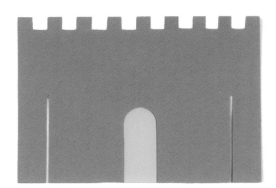

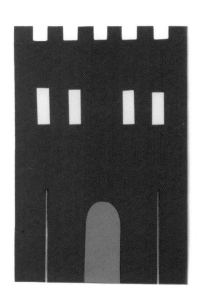

Each of the eight projects in this book are fun, easy-to-make
and will help you to build your crafting skills while
using your imagination to make wonderful things!

Every activity is an opportunity to decorate, use colour and design
your project in a way that makes it uniquely yours.

Why not show your friends how to make these projects too and share
them with each other? Seeing how other people use their imaginations is
a great way to get to know someone and find even more inspiration!

Always remember – safety first!

**Be sure to always let an adult know when you are about to use
scissors or glue, and always ask an adult for help when using a
craft knife – never use one on your own!**